A BEGINNER'S GUIDE TO SALTWATER AQUARIUMS

Learn About Saltwater Fish, Reef Tanks, & Different Species

JAKE BROWN

Copyright © 2021 Scott Matthews

All rights reserved. No part of this publication may be reproduced, distributed or transmitted in any form or by any means, including photocopying, recording, or other electronic or mechanical methods, without the prior written permission of the publisher, except in the case of brief quotations embodied in critical reviews and certain other non-commercial uses permitted by copyright law.

Trademarked names appear throughout this book. Rather than use a trademark symbol with every occurrence of a trademarked name, names are used in an editorial fashion, with no intention of infringement of the respective owner's trademark. The information in this book is distributed on an "as is" basis, without warranty. Although every precaution has been taken in the preparation of this work, neither the author nor the publisher shall have any liability to any person or entity with respect to any loss or damage caused or alleged to be caused directly or indirectly by the information contained in this book.

Contents

1. Chapter 1: Diving Into the World of Saltwater Aquariums — 1
2. Chapter 2: Planning Your Saltwater Aquarium — 3
3. Chapter 3: Setting Up Your Saltwater Aquarium — 5
4. Chapter 4: Understanding Water Chemistry for a Healthy Saltwater Aquarium — 11
5. Chapter 5: Choosing the Right Saltwater Fish and Invertebrates for Your Aquarium — 14
6. Chapter 6: Common Challenges in Your Saltwater Aquarium — 16
7. Chapter 7: Advanced Techniques for Maintaining a Thriving Saltwater Aquarium — 18
8. Chapter 8: Becoming a Part of the Aquarium Community — 20
9. Chapter 9: Troubleshooting Common Problems in Your Saltwater Aquarium — 22
10. Chapter 10: The Future of Saltwater Aquariums — 24

"Nothing good happens fast in a reef Tank". -unknown

Chapter 1: Diving Into the World of Saltwater Aquariums

It all started with a glimmering flash of color that caught your eye at the local pet store. You were drawn to the beautifully decorated aquarium, with its vibrant corals, exotic fish, and various underwater life. As you approached the tank, the salty ocean scent filled your nostrils, and you were captivated by the mesmerizing world that lay beyond the glass.

You had heard about saltwater aquariums before, but setting up and maintaining one seemed daunting. However, that initial spark of interest quickly turned into a flame of curiosity. You found yourself researching everything there was to know about saltwater aquariums.

In this book, we'll take you on a journey into the fascinating world of saltwater aquariums.

But before we dive, let's first talk about why people are drawn to saltwater aquariums in the first place.

Saltwater aquariums offer a unique glimpse into a world otherwise hidden from view. They allow you to bring a piece of the ocean into your home or office and experience the beauty and wonder of marine life up close. The colors, shapes, and movements of the fish, coral, and other creatures create a living art piece that can be both calming and mesmerizing to watch.

For many, maintaining a saltwater aquarium becomes a rewarding hobby that challenges them to learn about marine ecosystems, water chemistry, and animal behavior. It can provide a sense of accomplishment as you watch your aquarium thrive and its creatures flourish.

However, setting up and maintaining a saltwater aquarium has challenges. It requires a significant investment of time, effort, and money. It can also be complex and intimidating, especially for those new to the hobby.

But don't worry; we will be with you every step of the way, guiding you through the process and providing you with the knowledge and tools you need to succeed. So, let's roll up our sleeves and dive into the exciting world of saltwater aquariums.

Chapter 2: Planning Your Saltwater Aquarium

Now that you've decided to plunge into the world of saltwater aquariums, it's time to start planning. Planning is the key to success in setting up and maintaining a saltwater aquarium.

The first step in planning your aquarium is to choose the correct location. You'll want to find a spot in your home or office with a stable temperature and minimal fluctuations in lighting. Direct sunlight should be avoided because it can cause algae growth and temperature fluctuations.

Next, you'll need to determine the appropriate size of your aquarium. Consider the available space, as well as your budget and the type of marine life you want to keep. The bigger the aquarium, the more stable it will be and the more options you'll have regarding the species you can keep.

Once you've chosen the location and size of your aquarium, it's time to select the right equipment. A basic saltwater aquarium setup will include a tank, filtration system, heater, lighting, and a protein skimmer. You'll also need test kits for monitoring water parameters and various accessories, such as a thermometer, powerheads, and a hydrometer.

When selecting your equipment, it's crucial to invest in quality products. Cheap equipment can often cause more harm than good and cost you more in the long run. Do your research and ask for recommendations from experienced hobbyists.

Now that your location, size, and equipment are selected, it's time to set up your aquarium. This process involves installing and maintaining your equipment, preparing and adding saltwater to your aquarium, and adding live rock and substrate.

It's essential to take your time during the setup process and ensure everything is done correctly. Rushing can lead to mistakes that can harm your marine life and potentially cost you money in the long run.

In the next chapter, we'll dive into the specifics of setting up your saltwater aquarium and help you get your tank up and running smoothly. So, grab your coffee and let's get started!

Chapter 3: Setting Up Your Saltwater Aquarium

Setting up your saltwater aquarium is an exciting and crucial step in starting your marine adventure. A well-planned and executed setup will provide the foundation for a healthy and thriving aquarium.

The first step in setting up your saltwater aquarium is thoroughly cleaning your tank. This will remove any dust, debris, or residual substances that may have accumulated during manufacturing. Once the tank is clean, it's time to install the equipment.

The filtration system is essential for maintaining a stable and healthy environment for your marine life. It removes waste, excess nutrients, and harmful chemicals from the water. The type of filtration system you choose will depend on the size of your aquarium, the type of marine life you plan to keep, and your personal preference.

Regarding filtration options for saltwater aquariums, two of the most popular choices are canister filters and sumps. Both of these filtration systems have advantages and disadvantages, and which one you choose will depend on your individual needs and preferences.

A canister filter is a standalone filtration unit typically placed under or next to the aquarium. It operates by drawing water from the aquarium through an intake tube and passing it through various filter media, such as foam pads, mechanical filter media, biological media, and chemical media. The filtered water is returned to the aquarium through a spray bar or return hose.

One of the main advantages of using a canister filter is that it is a self-contained unit that is easy to install and maintain. It also allows for flexibility regarding the types of filter media that can be used, as you can customize the filter to your specific needs. However, canister filters can be bulky and take up space outside of the aquarium and may require periodic cleaning and maintenance to ensure optimal performance.

On the other hand, a sump is an additional chamber or tank located below the main aquarium and connected to it via an overflow box or other plumbing. The water from the aquarium flows into the sump, where it passes through various filter media and equipment, such as a protein skimmer, heater, and return pump. The filtered water is then returned to the aquarium through a return line.

One of the main advantages of using a sump is that it provides additional volume for filtration equipment, which can help increase the overall efficiency and effectiveness of the filtration system. It can also help to hide equipment, such as heaters and protein skimmers, from view, creating a more aesthetic look. However, sumps can be more complex to install and require more space underneath the aquarium.

They also require regular maintenance and cleaning and may require additional equipment, such as an overflow box or plumbing.

Ultimately, choosing between a canister filter and a sump will depend on your specific needs and preferences. Canister filters are typically easier to install and maintain, while sumps offer greater flexibility and increased filtration capabilities. It's important to consider factors such as space, budget, and desired level of filtration before deciding.

Next, you'll need to add your substrate and live rock. Substrate provides a natural base for your marine life to live on and helps to create a stable environment. Live rock, on the other hand, provides a natural filtration system and helps to create a healthy biological environment in your aquarium.

The substrate in a saltwater aquarium refers to the material, such as sand or crushed coral, placed on the bottom of the tank. Going bare bottom, on the other hand, means not using any substrate at all.

Both approaches have advantages and disadvantages, and the choice ultimately depends on personal preference and the needs of your aquarium.

Using substrate in a saltwater aquarium can help create a natural environment for the fish and other inhabitants and provide a surface for beneficial bacteria to grow. Sand, in particular, can also help maintain a stable pH level and provide a home for sand-dwelling creatures such as certain fish species and invertebrates. The substrate can also help hide unsightly equipment and debris, creating a more aesthetically pleasing appearance.

However, the substrate can also be challenging to clean and maintain, as waste and debris can become trapped in the sand, creating pockets of anaerobic bacteria that can release harmful gases. The substrate can also be a breeding ground for pests like bristle worms. Additionally, some species of fish and invertebrates may dig or burrow in the sand, potentially causing issues with the stability of structures such as rocks and coral.

Going bare bottom in a saltwater aquarium eliminates many potential issues associated with the substrate. It can make cleaning and maintenance more manageable, as there is no sand to trap waste and debris. It can also provide a more stable surface for structures such as rocks and coral and make it easier to control the water flow in the tank. Additionally, going bare bottom can create a more modern, minimalist look that some aquarists prefer.

However, going bare bottom can also be less natural looking. It may not provide the best environment for certain fish species and invertebrates. It can also make it more difficult for beneficial bacteria to colonize the tank, potentially leading to issues with water quality.

Ultimately, the decision to use substrate or go bare bottom in a saltwater aquarium comes down to personal preference and the specific needs of your tank. It's important to weigh the pros and cons of each approach and consider factors such as the species of fish and invertebrates you plan to keep, as well as your own maintenance preferences and aesthetic goals.

Once your substrate and live rock are in place, it's time to add saltwater. You can purchase pre-mixed saltwater from your local aquarium store or mix your own using a marine salt mix and purified water. It's essential to mix the saltwater properly and allow it to stabilize before adding it to your tank.

Steps for mixing your own saltwater at home.

1 Gather the necessary materials: You will need a large container (such as a food-grade plastic bucket) that can hold the amount of water needed for your aquarium, a heater, a powerhead or pump for mixing, and a high-quality aquarium salt mix.

2 Fill the container with water: Fill the container with clean RO (reverse osmosis) water. Use a thermometer to ensure the water is at the appropriate temperature for your aquarium (usually around 75-78°F / 23°C-25°C).

3 Add the salt mix: Add the appropriate amount to the water based on the manufacturer's instructions and the volume of water in the container. Use a reliable scale or measuring cup to ensure accuracy.

4 Mix the salt: Use a powerhead or pump to mix the salt and water thoroughly. You can also stir the mixture with a clean, long-handled spoon or another utensil. Aim for a consistent salinity level throughout the container, which can be measured using a hydrometer or refractometer.

5 Monitor the salinity level: Allow the salt mix to dissolve completely, then let the mixture sit for a few hours to stabilize. Measure the salinity level again and adjust as needed until you achieve the desired salinity level for your aquarium.

6 Use the saltwater: Once it has reached the appropriate salinity level and stabilized, it is ready for use in your aquarium. Slowly add the saltwater to your aquarium over several hours, monitoring the temperature and salinity levels as you go.

Using high-quality aquarium salt mix is essential, as using low-quality or inappropriate salt can harm your aquarium inhabitants. Additionally, it's a good idea to mix your saltwater for at least a day or two before you use it, as this allows any gases to escape and the mixture to stabilize. Finally, clean and sanitize your mixing container and equipment thoroughly after each use to prevent contamination.

After adding the saltwater, it's time to install your lighting and temperature control system. Proper lighting is crucial for the health and growth of your marine life. At the same time, temperature control is essential for maintaining a stable environment.

Finally, you'll need to add your marine life. It's important to start with a small number of fish and allow the environment to stabilize before adding more. Make sure to research the species you plan to add and ensure they are compatible with each other and with your environment.

Setting up your saltwater aquarium can be a challenging and time-consuming process, but the rewards are well worth the effort. In the next chapter, we'll cover the basics of water chemistry and help you understand how to maintain a stable and healthy environment for your marine life. So, let's dive in!

Chapter 4: Understanding Water Chemistry for a Healthy Saltwater Aquarium

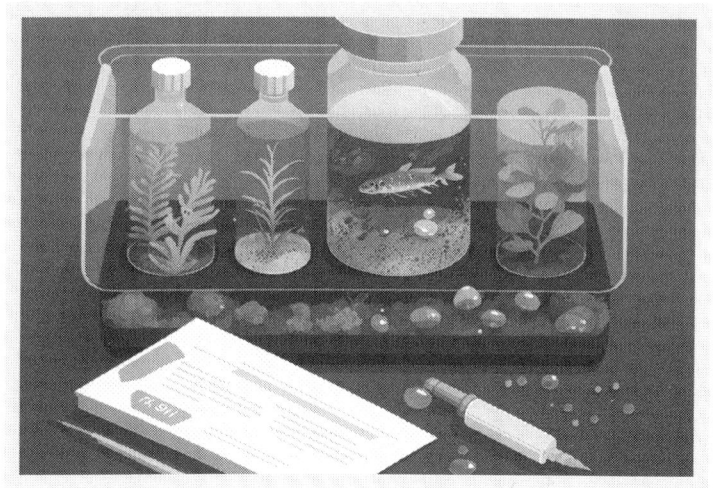

Water chemistry is the foundation of a healthy and thriving saltwater aquarium. Understanding the basics of water chemistry is essential for maintaining a stable and healthy environment for your marine life.

The nitrogen cycle is a critical process that occurs in every aquarium and is essential for maintaining a healthy and stable environment for fish and other aquatic life. Here is a brief overview of how the nitrogen cycle works in a saltwater aquarium:

1. Ammonia production: The first step in the nitrogen cycle is ammonia production. Ammonia is excreted by fish, leftover food, and decaying plant matter. Ammonia is highly toxic to fish and other aquatic life and can quickly build up in the aquarium.

2. Nitrosomonas bacteria convert ammonia to nitrite: The second step in the nitrogen cycle is the conversion of ammonia into nitrite. This process is carried out by beneficial bacteria known as Nitrosomonas. These bacteria break down the ammonia into nitrite through a process called nitrification.

3. Nitrobacter bacteria convert nitrite to nitrate: The next step in the nitrogen cycle is the conversion of nitrite into nitrate. This process is carried out by a different beneficial bacteria known as Nitrobacter. These bacteria convert the nitrite into nitrate through a process called nitrification.

4. Nitrate removal: While nitrate is less toxic than ammonia and nitrite, high nitrate levels can still harm fish and other aquatic life. Nitrate is typically removed from the aquarium through regular water changes or the use of special filtration systems such as protein skimmers.

5. Starting the cycle: In a new aquarium, the nitrogen cycle may take several weeks to establish as the beneficial bacteria populations grow. It's essential to test the water regularly to ensure that ammonia and nitrite levels are not reaching toxic levels. Some aquarists may add small amounts of fish slowly to help kick-start the cycle.

Understanding water chemistry is to test your water regularly. This will help you to monitor the levels of ammonia, nitrite, nitrate, pH, and other vital parameters in your aquarium. Test kits can be purchased from your local aquarium store or online.

Ammonia and nitrite are harmful to your marine life and can lead to disease and death if not controlled. These chemicals are produced by fish waste and decaying organic matter. Nitrate, on the other hand, is less harmful but can still cause problems in high concentrations.

The pH level of your aquarium water is also vital for the health of your marine life. The ideal pH range for most saltwater fish and invertebrates is between 8.0 and 8.4.

You'll need to perform regular water changes to maintain a healthy environment. This helps to remove excess nutrients and chemicals and replenish the necessary minerals and trace elements in your aquarium. The amount of water you need to change depends on the size of your aquarium and the number of fish you have.

In addition to water changes, you'll need to maintain your equipment regularly. This includes cleaning your filters, protein skimmer, and other equipment to ensure they function correctly.

Finally, it's important to keep an eye on your marine life and watch for signs of disease or stress. Common signs of disease include lethargy, loss of appetite, and abnormal behavior. If you notice any of these signs, it's crucial to take action quickly to prevent the spread of the disease.

Understanding water chemistry is essential for maintaining a healthy and thriving saltwater aquarium. Regular testing, water changes, and equipment maintenance will help you create a stable marine life environment. In the next chapter, we'll explore the different types of saltwater fish and invertebrates and help you choose the suitable species for your aquarium. So, let's dive in!

Chapter 5: Choosing the Right Saltwater Fish and Invertebrates for Your Aquarium

Choosing the right saltwater fish and invertebrates is an exciting and essential step in creating a beautiful and thriving aquarium. There are many different species of saltwater fish and invertebrates to choose from, each with unique characteristics and requirements.

Before choosing your marine life, it's important to consider the size of your aquarium and the compatibility of the species you plan to keep. Some species are more aggressive than others and may not get along well with certain types of fish or invertebrates.

When it comes to saltwater fish, there are many different types to choose from, including reef-safe fish, aggressive fish, and schooling fish. Some popular choices for beginner aquariums include clownfish, damselfish, and goby.

In addition to fish, many aquarium enthusiasts choose to keep invertebrates in their aquarium. These can include shrimp, crabs, snails, and corals. It's essential to research the specific requirements of each species before adding them to your aquarium.

When choosing your marine life, it's also important to consider their feeding habits. Some species require a specific type of food, while others are more flexible in their diet.

To ensure the health and wellbeing of your marine life, it's crucial to provide them with a stable and healthy environment. This includes maintaining proper water chemistry, providing adequate filtration and lighting, and keeping a close eye on their behavior and health.

Choosing the right saltwater fish and invertebrates can be a challenging and rewarding experience. With proper research and planning, you can create a beautiful and thriving aquarium that brings joy and tranquility to your home or office. In the next chapter, we'll explore common challenges and how to troubleshoot them to keep your aquarium healthy and happy. So, let's dive in!

Chapter 6: Common Challenges in Your Saltwater Aquarium

Maintaining a saltwater aquarium can be a rewarding and fulfilling experience, but it's not without its challenges. Even with the best care and attention, issues can arise in your aquarium that can threaten the health and wellbeing of your marine life.

One common challenge that aquarium enthusiasts face is algae growth. Algae can be unsightly and can also consume excess nutrients in your aquarium, which can lead to imbalances in your water chemistry. To combat algae growth, it's important to maintain proper lighting levels and to perform regular water changes to remove excess nutrients. You can add algae-eating fish or invertebrates to your aquarium, such as snails or hermit crabs.

Another common challenge is the buildup of waste and debris in your aquarium. This can lead to poor water quality and increased ammonia and nitrite levels. To prevent waste buildup, it's important to regularly clean your aquarium and equipment, including your filters, protein skimmer, and substrate.

Marine life diseases and parasites can also be a challenge in a saltwater aquarium. Common signs of disease include lethargy, loss of appetite, and abnormal behavior. To prevent the spread of disease, it's important to quarantine new fish and invertebrates before introducing them to your aquarium, and to maintain good water quality and hygiene.

Finally, equipment failure can also be a challenge in a saltwater aquarium. To prevent this, it's essential to regularly maintain and check your equipment to ensure it functions correctly. It's also a good idea to keep backup equipment on hand in case of a malfunction.

Maintaining a healthy and thriving saltwater aquarium requires patience, dedication, and attention to detail. By understanding common challenges and how to troubleshoot them, you can create a beautiful and thriving aquarium that brings joy and tranquility to your home or office. In the next chapter, we'll explore some advanced tips and techniques for taking your saltwater aquarium to the next level. So, let's dive in!

Chapter 7: Advanced Techniques for Maintaining a Thriving Saltwater Aquarium

Once you've mastered the basics of maintaining a saltwater aquarium, you may be interested in taking your skills to the next level. There are a variety of advanced techniques and strategies that can help you create a truly thriving and beautiful aquarium.

One advanced technique is reef aquascaping, which involves creating a visually stunning and biologically diverse environment for your marine life. This can involve using live rock, live sand, and various corals to create a natural-looking reef environment.

Another advanced technique is using specialized equipment, such as dosing pumps, reactors, and ozone generators. These tools can help you maintain optimal water chemistry and nutrient levels in your aquarium, which can promote the growth and health of your marine life.

In addition to advanced techniques, there are a variety of specialized species and types of marine life that you may be interested in keeping in your aquarium. For example, some aquarium enthusiasts specialize in keeping rare or exotic species of coral, while others focus on breeding and raising their own fish and invertebrates.

As you explore advanced techniques and specialized species, it's essential to continue to prioritize the health and wellbeing of your marine life. This means maintaining stable water chemistry, providing adequate filtration and lighting, and monitoring the behavior and health of your fish and invertebrates.

Maintaining a thriving saltwater aquarium can be a lifelong passion and journey. By continuing to learn and grow in your knowledge and skills, you can create a truly unique and beautiful aquarium that brings joy and tranquility to your home or office. In the final chapter, we'll explore some tips for sharing your love of aquariums with others and becoming a part of the larger aquarium community. So, let's dive in!

Chapter 8: Becoming a Part of the Aquarium Community

One of the joys of maintaining a saltwater aquarium is the opportunity to connect with others who share your passion. There is a vibrant and welcoming community of aquarium enthusiasts, with a variety of clubs, forums, and events where you can connect with like-minded individuals.

Joining a local aquarium club can be a great way to meet other aquarium enthusiasts in your area. Clubs often hold regular meetings and events where you can learn new skills, share knowledge, and connect with others who share your passion.

Online forums and social media groups can also be a valuable resource for connecting with other aquarium enthusiasts. These forums provide a platform for asking questions, sharing photos and videos, and getting advice and support from others who are passionate about saltwater aquariums.

In addition to connecting with other hobbyists, there are also a variety of aquarium-related events and competitions that you may be interested in attending or participating in. These events can be a great way to learn more about the latest trends and techniques in the hobby and to meet and connect with other aquarium enthusiasts from around the world.

Becoming a part of the aquarium community can be an enriching experience. By connecting with others who share your passion, you can learn new skills, discover new ideas, and gain a deeper appreciation for the beauty and complexity of the marine world.

In conclusion, maintaining a saltwater aquarium is a rewarding and fulfilling hobby that can bring joy and tranquility to your home or office. Following the tips and strategies outlined in this guide, you can create a beautiful and thriving aquarium that brings you years of enjoyment. And by connecting with the larger aquarium community, you can deepen your knowledge and appreciation of this fascinating hobby. So, happy fishkeeping, and may your aquarium always be full of life and beauty!

Chapter 9: Troubleshooting Common Problems in Your Saltwater Aquarium

Even the most experienced aquarium enthusiasts may encounter problems with their saltwater aquarium from time to time. However, with the proper knowledge and strategies, you can quickly and effectively troubleshoot and solve many common problems.

One of the most common issues saltwater aquarium owners encounter is algae growth. This can occur when nutrient levels in the aquarium are too high or when lighting levels are too strong. To address this issue, you may need to adjust your feeding and water change schedule or adjust the intensity and duration of your lighting.

Another common issue is the presence of harmful organisms, such as parasites or bacteria, in your aquarium. Suppose you notice unusual behavior or symptoms in your fish or invertebrates, such as lethargy, loss of appetite, or visible signs of disease. In that case, it's crucial to take action quickly to address the issue. This may involve using medications or other treatments to eliminate harmful organisms and promote the health of your marine life.

Water quality issues, such as high levels of nitrates, can also be a concern in saltwater aquariums. To address this issue, you may need to increase the frequency and volume of your water changes or use specialized equipment such as a protein skimmer or denitrifying filter to help remove excess nutrients from the water.

Other common problems in saltwater aquariums include equipment malfunctions, temperature fluctuations, and introduction of incompatible species or organisms. By staying vigilant and responding quickly to any issues that arise, you can help ensure the health and wellbeing of your marine life.

In conclusion, while owning a saltwater aquarium can be a rewarding and enjoyable experience, it's important to be prepared to address common problems that may arise. By staying informed and taking prompt action, you can help ensure your aquarium's long-term health and beauty. So, be proactive and stay vigilant, and may your aquarium always be a source of joy and tranquility.

Chapter 10: The Future of Saltwater Aquariums

As the world continues to change and evolve, the future of saltwater aquariums is also undergoing significant transformation. Technological advancements in equipment and materials have made it easier and more accessible than ever before to create and maintain beautiful and healthy saltwater aquariums.

One trend likely to continue is the increased use of automation and smart technology in saltwater aquariums. From automated lighting and feeding systems to advanced monitoring and control systems, these technologies can make it easier and more convenient for aquarium enthusiasts to maintain their aquariums.

Another trend likely to continue is the growing focus on sustainability and environmental responsibility in the saltwater aquarium hobby. This includes a greater emphasis on responsible sourcing, aquaculture of marine life, and efforts to reduce waste and conserve resources.

Additionally, there is a growing awareness of the importance of the conservation and protection of marine ecosystems, and many aquarium enthusiasts are becoming more involved in efforts to promote these goals. By working together with conservation organizations and other stakeholders, aquarium enthusiasts can help ensure that the beauty and diversity of the marine world are preserved for future generations to enjoy.

In conclusion, the future of saltwater aquariums is bright and promising. As technology and knowledge continue to advance, the possibilities for creating and maintaining beautiful and healthy aquariums will only continue to expand. And by staying informed, engaged, and environmentally responsible, we can help ensure that the beauty and wonder of the marine world will continue to inspire and enrich our lives for many years to come.

Made in United States
Troutdale, OR
06/13/2025

32104792R00020